Prayers to Expel

the Evil Spirits

Nihil Obstat:
Rev. Basil Stegmann, O.S.B. Censor Librorum
Imprimatur:
Jos. F. Busch
Episcopus St. Clodoaldi
September 20, 1945

Prayers to Expel

the Evil Spirits

(EXORCISM)

The Prayers of Exorcism Begin With the Litany of The Saints

Lord have mercy on us.
Christ have mercy on us.
Lord have mercy on us.
Christ, hear us,
Christ, Graciously hear us,
God the Father of heaven. *Have mercy on us.*
God the Son, Redeemer of the world, *Have mercy on us.*
God the Holy Ghost, *Have mercy on us.*
Holy Trinity, One God, *Have mercy on us.*
Holy Mary, *Pray for us!*
Holy Mother of God, *Pray for us!*
Holy Virgin of Virgins, *Pray for us!*
St. Michael, *Pray for us!*
St. Gabriel, *Pray for us!*
St. Raphael, *Pray for us!*
All ye holy angels and archangels, *Pray for us!*
All ye holy orders of blessed spirits, *Pray for us!*
St. John Baptist, St. Joseph, *Pray for us!*
All ye holy patriarchs and prophets, *Pray for us!*
St. Peter, *Pray for us!*
St. Paul, *Pray for us!*
St. Andrew, *Pray for us!*
St. James, *Pray for us!*
St. John, *Pray for us!*
St. Thomas, *Pray for us!*
St. James, *Pray for us!*
St. Philip, *Pray for us!*
St. Bartholomew, *Pray for us!*
St. Matthew, *Pray for us!*
St. Simon, *Pray for us!*
St. Thaddeus, *Pray for us!*
St. Mathias, *Pray for us!*
St. Barnabas, *Pray for us!*
St. Luke, *Pray for us!*

St. Mark, *Pray for us!*
All ye holy apostles and evangelists, *Pray for us!*
All ye holy disciples of the Lord, *Pray for us!*
All ye holy innocents, *Pray for us!*
St. Stephen, *Pray for us!*
St. Laurence, *Pray for us!*
St. Vincent, *Pray for us!*
SS. Fabian and Sebastian, *Pray for us!*
SS. John and Paul, *Pray for us!*
SS. Cosmos and Damian, *Pray for us!*
SS. Gervase and Protase, *Pray for us!*
All ye holy martyrs, *Pray for us!*
St. Sylvester, *Pray for us!*
St. Gregory, *Pray for us!*
St. Ambrose, *Pray for us!*
St. Augustine, *Pray for us!*
St. Jerome, *Pray for us!*
St. Martin, *Pray for us!*
St. Nicholas, *Pray for us!*
All ye holy bishops and confessors, *Pray for us!*
All ye holy doctors, *Pray for us!*
St. Anthony, *Pray for us!*
St. Benedict, *Pray for us!*
St. Bernard, *Pray for us!*
St. Dominic, *Pray for us!*
St. Francis, *Pray for us!*
All ye holy priests and levites, *Pray for us!*
All ye holy monks and hermits, *Pray for us!*
St. Mary Magdalen, *Pray for us!*
St. Agatha, *Pray for us!*
St. Lucy, *Pray for us!*
St. Agnes, *Pray for us!*
St. Cecilia, *Pray for us!*
St. Catherine, *Pray for us!*
St. Anastasia, *Pray for us!*
All ye holy virgins and widows, *Pray for us!*

V. All ye holy saints of God,

R. Intercede for us.
V. Be merciful,
R. Spare us, O Lord!
V. Be merciful,
R. Graciously hear us, O Lord!

From all evil, *O Lord deliver us.*
From all sin, *O Lord deliver us.*
From Thy wrath, *O Lord deliver us.*
From a sudden and unprovided death, *O Lord deliver us.*
From the snares of the devil, *O Lord deliver us.*
From anger, hatred and all ill will, *O Lord deliver us.*
From the spirit of fornication, *O Lord deliver us.*
From lightning and tempest, *O Lord deliver us.*
From the scourge of earthquake, *O Lord deliver us.*
From pestilence, famine and war, *O Lord deliver us.*
From everlasting death, *O Lord deliver us.*
Through the Mystery of Thy holy Incarnation. *O Lord deliver us.*
Through Thy coming, Through Thy nativity, *O Lord deliver us.*
Through Thy baptism and holy fasting, *O Lord deliver us.*
Through Thy cross and passion, *O Lord deliver us.*
Through Thy death and burial, *O Lord deliver us.*
Through Thy holy resurrection, *O Lord deliver us.*
Through Thine admirable ascension, *O Lord deliver us.*
Through the coming of the Holy Ghost, the Paraclete,
    O Lord deliver us.
In the day of judgment, *O Lord deliver us.*
We sinners, *We beseech Thee, hear us.*
That Thou wouldst spare us, *We beseech Thee, hear us.*
That Thou wouldst pardon us, *We beseech Thee, hear us.*
That Thou wouldst bring us to true penance,
    We beseech Thee, hear us.
That Thou wouldst deign to govern and preserve Thy Holy Church,
    We beseech Thee, hear us.
That Thou wouldst deign to preserve our apostolic prelate and all
    orders of the Church in holy religion,
    We beseech Thee, hear us.
That Thou wouldst deign to humble the enemies of Thy Holy

Church, *We beseech Thee, hear us.*
That Thou wouldst deign to give peace and true concord to Christian rulers and princes. *We beseech Thee, hear us.*
That Thou wouldst deign to grant peace and unity to all Christian people, *We beseech Thee, hear us.*
That Thou wouldst deign to bring back all the erring to the unity of the Church, and return all unbelievers to the light of the Gospel, *We beseech Thee, hear us.*
That Thou wouldst deign to confirm and preserve us in Thy holy service, *We beseech Thee, hear us.*
That Thou wouldst lift up our minds to heavenly desires, *We beseech Thee, hear us.*
That Thou wouldst render eternal blessings to all our benefactors, *We beseech Thee, hear us.*
That Thou wouldst deliver our souls and the souls of our brethren, relatives and benefactors, from eternal damnation, *We beseech Thee, hear us.*
That Thou wouldst deign to give and preserve the fruits of the earth, *We beseech Thee, hear us.*
That Thou wouldst deign to grant eternal rest to all the faithful departed, *We beseech Thee, hear us.*
That Thou wouldst deign graciously to hear us.
We beseech Thee, hear us.
Son of God, *We beseech Thee, hear us.*

V. Lamb of God, who takest away the sins of the world,
R. Spare us, O Lord,
V. Lamb of God, who takest away the sins of the world,
R. Graciously hear us, O Lord,
V. Lamb of God, who takest away the sins of the world,
R. Have mercy on us.
Christ hear us,
V. Christ graciously hear us.
Lord have mercy on us.
Christ have mercy on us.
Lord have mercy on us.

(The following translation of the prayers of exorcism has not been approved, and is for private use, only.)

PRAYER

Remember not, O Lord, our offenses, nor those of our parents; and take not revenge for our sins.

Our Father, etc.

V. And lead us not into temptation,
R. But deliver us from evil. Amen.

PSALM 53

Save me, O God, by Thy name; and judge me in Thy strength.
O God, hear my prayers; give ear to the words of my mouth.
For strangers have risen up against me; and the mighty have sought
    after my soul, and they have not set God before their eyes.
For behold God is my helper; and the Lord is the protector of my
    soul.
Turn back the evils upon my enemies: and cut them off in Thy
    Truth.
I will freely sacrifice to Thee; and will give praise, O God to Thy
    Name; because it is good.
For Thou halt delivered me out of all trouble, and my eye bath
    looked down upon my enemies.
Glory be to the Father, and to the Son, and to the Holy Ghost;
As it was in the beginning, is now, and ever shall be, world without
    end. R. Amen.

V. Save Thy servant (handmaid),
R. O My God who trusteth in Thee.
V. Be unto him (her) O Lord, a tower of strength,
R. From the face of the enemy.
V. Let not the enemy prevail against him (her)
R. Nor the son of iniquity have power to hurt him (her).
V. Send him (her) help O Lord, from Thy holy place,
R. And from Sion protect him (her).
V. O Lord, hear my prayer,
R. And let my cry come unto Thee.

V. The Lord be with you,
R. And with thy spirit.

LET US PRAY

O God, whose property is always to have mercy and to spare, receive our humble petition; that this, Thy servant (handmaid), who is bound by the chains of sin, may, by the compassion of Thy Goodness, mercifully be absolved. Holy Lord, Father Almighty, Eternal God, Father of Our Lord Jesus Christ, Who hast consigned that tyrannical refugee and apostate to the fires of hell, and Who has sent Thine Only-begotten into this world that He might crush the roaring lion, come quickly and hasten to save mankind, made to Thy Image and Likeness, ✠ from ruin and from the noon-day devil. Put, O Lord, Thy fear upon the beast who destroys Thy vineyard. Give confidence to Thy servants, that they may fight bravely against the most wicked dragon, so that he may not despise those who confide in Thee; and that he may not say, as he has already said, through Pharaoh; "I know not God, neither will I release Israel."

Let Thy powerful hand force him to depart from Thy servant (handmaid) that he may not presume to hold him (her) captive longer whom Thou hast deigned to make to Thy Image, and redeem by Thy Son, who liveth and reigneth with Thee and the Holy Ghost, throughout the ages of ages. Amen.

(THE DEMON IS THEN ADDRESSED AS FOLLOWS)

I command you, unclean spirit, whomsoever you may be, and all your associates, who are obsessing this servant of God, that by the mysteries of the Incarnation, Passion, Resurrection and Ascension of Our Lord Jesus Christ, by the sending of the Holy Ghost, and by the coming of the same Lord for the judgment; that you tell me your name, the day and hour of your departure, by some sign; and that, in all things, you obey me completely, although an unworthy minister of God, and that you harm not this creature of God, nor the bystanders, nor their possessions.

(THEN THE FOLLOWING GOSPELS, OR AT LEAST ONE OF THEM, IS READ OVER THE OBSESSED ONE.)

THE BEGINNING OF THE HOLY GOSPEL ACCORDING TO ST. JOHN

In the beginning was the Word, and the Word was with God, and the Word was God. The same was in the beginning with God. All things were made by Him, and without Him was made nothing that was made. In Him was life, and the life was the light of men, and the light shineth in darkness, and the darkness did not comprehend it. There was a man sent from God whose name was John. This man came for a witness to give testimony of the light, that all men might believe through him. He was not the light, but was to give testimony of the light. That was the true light which enlighteneth every man that cometh into the world. He was in the world, and the world was made by Him, and the world knew Him not. He came unto His own, and His own received Him not. But as many as received Him, to them He gave power to become the sons of God; to them that believe in His name; who are born, not of blood, nor of the will of the flesh, nor of the will of man, but of God. AND THE WORD WAS MADE FLESH and dwelt among us, and we saw His glory, the glory as of the Only-Begotten of the Father, full of grace and truth.

THE HOLY GOSPEL ACCORDING TO ST. MARK (16, 5-18)

At that time Jesus said to them: "Go into the whole world and preach the Gospel to every creature. He who believes and is baptized shall be saved, but he who does not believe shall be condemned. And these signs shall attend those who believe: in My Name they shall cast out devils; they shall speak new tongues; they shall take up serpents, and if they drink any deadly thing, it shall not hurt them; they shall lay their hands on the sick, and they shall recover.

THE HOLY GOSPEL ACCORDING TO ST. LUKE (10, 17-20)

At that time, the seventy-two returned with joy, saying: "Lord, even the devils are subject to us in Thy Name." But He said to them: "I was watching satan fall as lightning from heaven. Behold, I have given you power to tread upon serpents and scorpions, and over all the power of the enemy, and nothing shall hurt you. Do not rejoice in this, that the spirits are subject to you, but rejoice in this, that your names are written in heaven."

THE HOLY GOSPEL ACCORDING TO ST. LUKE (11, 14-22)

At that time Jesus was casting out a devil and the same was dumb; and when He had cast out the devil, the dumb man spoke. And the crowds marvelled. But some of them said, "By Beelzebub, the prince of devils, he casts out devils". But others, to test Him, demanded from Him a sign from heaven. But He, seeing their thoughts, said to them: "Every kingdom divided against itself is brought to desolation, and house upon house shall fall. If, then, satan is divided against himself, how shall his kingdom stand? Because you say that I cast out devils by Beelzebub, by whom do your children cast them out? Therefore, they shall be your judges. But if I cast out devils by the finger of God, doubtless the kingdom of God has come upon you. When a strong man, armed, guards his courtyard, his property is undisturbed. But if a stronger than he attack and overcome him, he will take away all his armor upon which he was depending."

V. O Lord, hear my prayer,
R. And let my cry come unto Thee.
V. The Lord be with you
R. And with thy spirit.

LET US PRAY

Omnipotent Lord, Word of God the Father, Jesus Christ, God and Master of all creatures, Who hast given to Thy holy Apostles the power of treading on serpents and scorpions, Who among Thy other wonderful precepts hast deigned to say: "Begone demons!" by virtue of which satan fell like lightning from heaven; I humbly invoke Thy Holy Name with fear and trembling, That Thou mayest give to me, Thy most unworthy servant, a remission of all my sins, a constant faith and such power that, fortified by the strength of Thy arm, I may attack this cruel demon confidently and with safety. I ask this through Thee, Jesus Christ Our Lord, Who art to come to judge the living and the dead, and the world by fire. Amen.

V. Behold the Cross of the Lord, flee bands of enemies.
R. The Lion of the Tribe of Juda, the offspring of David, hath conquered.
V. O Lord, hear my prayer,
R. And let my cry come unto Thee.
V. The Lord be with you.
R. And with thy spirit.

LET US PRAY

O God, the Father of Our Lord Jesus Christ, I invoke Thy Holy Name, and humbly beg Thy mercy; that Thou mayest deign to grant me help against this and every evil spirit, who molests this Thy creature. Through the same Christ Our Lord. Amen.

EXORCISM

I drive you forth, most unclean spirit, every invader, every spectre, every legion of the enemy; in the Name of our Lord Jesus ✠ Christ. Be rooted out and flee from this creature of God. May He command you, Who ordered you down from the supernal heights of Heaven to the uttermost depths of the earth. May He, Who rules the seasons, the winds and the tempest, command you. Hear, therefore, and fear, Satan, enemy of faith, adversary of the human race, author of death, destroyer of life, fugitive from justice, root of evil, fomenter of vice, seducer of man, betrayer of nations, instigator of envy, font of avarice, cause of discord, producer of pain. Why do you stand and resist when you know that Christ the Lord has destroyed your wicked ways? Fear Him, Who was sacrificed in Isaac, sold in Joseph, slain in the lamb, crucified in man, and thus became the victor over hell. Depart, therefore, in the Name of the Father ✠ and of the Son ✠ and of the Holy Ghost. ✠ Give place to the Holy Spirit through this sign of the Holy ✠ Cross of our Lord Jesus Christ: Who, with the Father and the same Holy Ghost, liveth and reigneth, one God, world without end, Amen.

V. O Lord hear my prayer,
R. And let my cry come unto Thee.

V. The Lord be with you.
R. And with thy spirit.

LET US PRAY

O God, Creator and Defender of the human race, Who halt formed man to Thine Own Likeness, look upon this, Thy servant, N. N., who is sought by the deceits of the unclean spirit; whom the old enemy, the ancient adversary of the earth, surrounds with the horror of fright, stupefies in mind, disturbs with terror, and harasses with restless fear. Repel, O Lord, the power of the devil. Remove his treachery and deceitful snares. May the impious tempter flee far away. May Thy servant be protected by the Sign t of Thy Name, and be safe both in soul and in body. Guard Thou this ✠ breast; rule Thou this ✠ body, confirm Thou this ✠ heart. May the temptations of the hostile power vanish from the mind. Grant, O Lord, by the invocation of Thy most Holy Name, that he, who until now has terrified others may flee in terror and depart vanquished; and that this, Thy servant, may scrve Thee with a strong heart and a sincere mind. Through Christ Our Lord. Amen.

EXORCISM

I adjure you, ancient serpent, by the Judge of the living and the dead, by your Maker, by the Maker of the world, by Him Who has power to cast you into hell; that you depart in haste, with all the forces of your fury, from this servant of God, who has recourse to the bosom of the Church. I adjure you again ✠ (on forehead) not by my weakness, but by the power of the Holy Ghost, that you leave this servant of God, N. N. whom the Omnipotent God has made to His own Image. Give way, therefore, give way, not to me, but to the minister of Christ. May His power force you, Who has subjected you to His Cross. Fear His arm, Who overcame the groanings of hell and who led souls to light. Fear the human body ✠ (on forehead). Dread the image of God ✠ (on breast). Resist not, nor delay your departure from this person, for it has pleased Christ to dwell in man; and do not presume to despise me, although you know me to be a sinner. God commands you. ✠ The Majesty of Christ commands you. ✠ God the Father commands you. ✠ God the Son commands you. ✠ God the Holy Ghost commands you. ✠ The Sacrament of the Holy Cross commands you. ✠ The faith of the holy Apostles, Peter and Paul, and all the Saints, commands you. ✠ The blood of the Martyrs commands you. ✠ The constancy of the confessors commands you. ✠ The pious intercession of all the Saints commands you. ✠ The power of the mysteries of the Christian faith commands you. ✠ Depart, therefore, transgressor, depart seducer, full of deceit and treachery, enemy of virtue and persecutor of the innocent. Give place, O most cruel one, give place, O most impious one, give place to Christ, in Whom you have found none of your works; Who has stripped you, destroyed your kingdom, left you bound and conquered, and destroyed your possessions; Who has cast you into exterior darkness where eternal ruin is prepared for you and your angels. But why do you stubbornly resist? Why do you recklessly oppose? You are guilty before Almighty God, Whose laws you have transgressed. You are guilty before His Son, Our Lord Jesus Christ, Whom you have dared to tempt, and presumed to crucify. You are guilty before the human race, to whom by your persuasion you have administered the poison of death.

I adjure you, therefore, most wicked dragon, in the Name of the Immaculate ✠ Lamb, Who walked on the asp and the basilisk, Who has trampled under foot the lion and the dragon, that you leave this person ✠ (the sign of the cross is made on the forehead), and depart from the Church of God ✠ (the sign of the cross is made over those present). Tremble and flee at the invocation of the Name of the Lord, Whom hell fears, to Whom the Virtues, Powers, and Dominations of Heaven are subject, Whom the Cherubim and Seraphim unceasingly praise, saying: "Holy, Holy, Holy! Lord God of Hosts!"

The Word made ✠ Flesh commands you. He Who was born of the Virgin ✠ commands you. Jesus ✠ of Nazareth commands you; Who, when you despised His disciples, ordered you to depart from man, humbled and prostrate; in Whose presence, when He had cast you forth from man, you did not even dare to enter a herd of swine. Now, I adjure you in His Name ✠ to depart from this man (woman) whom He has made. It is hard for you to resist. ✠ It is hard for you to kick against the goad. ✠ The later you depart, the greater your punishment grows, because you do not despise man, but Him Who rules the living and the dead, and Who will come to judge the living and the dead, and the world by fire. Amen.

V. O Lord hear my prayer.
R. And let my cry come unto Thee.
V. The Lord be with you.
R. And with thy spirit.

LET US PRAY

God of Heaven, God of earth, God of Angels, God of Archangels, God of Patriarchs, God of Prophets, God of Apostles, God of Martyrs, God of Virgins, O God Who hast the power to give life after death and rest after work, because there is no other God than Thee, nor can there be any other true God except Thee, the Creator of Heaven and earth, Who art true King, and Whose reign will never end; prostrate before Thy Glorious Majesty, I humbly beg that Thou wouldst deign to free this, Thy servant, from unclean spirits, Through Christ Our Lord. Amen.

EXORCISM

I adjure you, therefore, every most unclean spirit, every phantom, every invasion of satan, in the Name of Jesus Christ ✠ of Nazareth, Who after John's baptism was led into the desert and conquered you on your own ground, that you cease to attack man whom God has formed from the slime of the earth for His Own Glory; and fear not human frailty in miserable man, but rather the Image of the Omnipotent God. Give place, therefore, to God, ✠ Who by Moses, His servant, submerged you and your malice, in Pharaoh and his army, in the depths of the sea. Give place to God ✠ Who has driven you with spiritual canticles from King Saul by His most faithful servant, David. Give place to God ✠ Who has damned you in the traitor Judas Iscariot. He will afflict you with divine scourges ✠ in Whose presence you and your legions have tremblingly cried out, "What have we to do with Thee, Jesus, Son of the Most High? Hast Thou come here to torment us before the time?" May He force you to depart with perpetual fires, Who at the end of time, is to say to sinners: "Depart from Me, you cursed, into the eternal fire which is prepared for the devil and his angels!" May the never-dying worms torment you, O wretched one, and all your angels. An unquenchable fire is prepared for you and for your angels, because you are the master of wretchedness, the author of incest, the chief of desecrators, the teacher of wickedness, the doctor of heretics, the inventor of all obscenity. Depart, therefore, impious ✠ spirit, depart ✠ wicked spirit, depart with all your perversity; because God desires man to be His temple. Why do you linger here? Give honor to God, the Almighty Father ✠ before Whom every knee bends. Give place to the Lord Jesus Christ ✠ Who has shed His most precious Blood for man. Give place to the Holy Ghost, ✠ Who, through His blessed Apostle Peter, has manifestly prostrated you in Simon the magician, Who condemned your lying in Ananias and Saphira, Who humiliated you in King Herod when he refused to give honor to God, Who, through His Apostle Paul, has stricken you with blindness in the person of the magician Elyma, and through the same Apostle has commanded you to go out from Pythonissa. Depart, therefore, now, ✠ depart, seducer. ✠ The desert is your home, the serpent your dwelling; be humbled and prostrate. There is now no time for delay. Behold the Lord, the Ruler, is fast approaching. A fire will burn before Him, and will precede Him, and will burn all His surrounding enemies. Although you have deluded men, you cannot mock God. He, in Whose sight nothing is hidden, will cast you forth. He, to Whose power all things are subject, will expel you. He will cast you forth, Who has prepared an eternal hell for you and for your angels, from Whose mouth will come a sharpened sword, Who is to come to judge the living and the dead, and the world by fire. Amen.

(All of the above, according to the need, may be repeated until the obsessed one is entirely freed. Also, it helps much to repeat the Our Father, the Hail Mary and the Creed, as well as other prayers and psalms as indicated in the ritual).

PRAYER AFTER LIBERATION

We pray Thee, Almighty God, that the spirit of iniquity may have no more power over this servant (handmaid) of Thine; but that he may fly in fear and may not return. By Thy command, O Lord, may the goodness and peace of Our Lord Jesus Christ, through Whom we have been redeemed, enter into him (her); and may we not fear any evil because the Lord is with us; Who lives and reigns with Thee, in union with the Holy Ghost, throughout all the ages of ages.

EXORCISM AGAINST SATAN AND THE REBELLIOUS ANGELS

Published by order of His Holiness, Pope Leo XIII, (Translation)

PRAYER TO ST. MICHAEL, THE ARCHANGEL

Glorious Prince of the Celestial Host, St. Michael the Archangel, defend us in the conflict which we have to sustain against principalities and powers, against the rulers of the world of this darkness, against the spirits of wickedness in high places. Come to the rescue of men whom God has created to His Image and Likeness and whom He has redeemed at a great price from the tyranny of the devil. It is thou whom Holy Church venerates as her guardian and her protector; thou whom the Lord has charged to conduct redeemed souls into heaven. Pray, therefore, the God of Peace to subdue Satan beneath our feet that he may no longer retain men captive nor do injury to the Church. Present our prayers to the Most High, that without delay they may draw His mercy down upon us. Seize "the dragon, the old serpent, which is the devil and Satan," bind him and cast him into the bottomless pit . . . "that he (may) no longer seduce the nations."

EXORCISM

In the Name of Jesus Christ, our Lord and Saviour, strengthened by the intercession of the Immaculate Virgin Mary, Mother of God, of Blessed Michael the Archangel, of the Blessed Apostles Peter and Paul, and all the Saints, and powerful in the holy authority of our ministry, we confidently undertake t o repulse t h e attacks and deceits of the devil.

PSALM 67

Let God arise, let His enemies be scattered; let them that hate Him flee before Him. "As smoke vanisheth. so let them vanish away: as wax melteth before the fire so let the wicked perish at the presence of God."

Behold the Cross of the Lord, flee bands of enemies.

R. The Lion of the tribe of Juda, the Offspring of David, hath conquered.
Let Thy mercy, O Lord, be upon us.
R. As we have hoped in Thee.

We drive you, from us, whoever you may be, unclean spirits, satanic powers, infernal invaders, wicked legions, assemblies and sects; in the Name and by virtue of Our Lord Jesus Christ, ✠ may you be snatched away and driven from the Church of God and from the souls redeemed by the Precious Blood of the Divine Lamb. ✠ Cease by your audacity, cunning serpent, to delude the human race, to persecute the Church, to torment God's elect, and to sift them as wheat. ✠ This is the command made by the Most High God, ✠ with Whom in your haughty insolence you still pretend to be equal, the God "Who will have all men to be saved and to come to the knowledge of the truth." God the Father commands you; ✠ God the Son commands you; ✠ God the Holy Ghost commands you; ✠ Christ commands you, the Eternal Word of God made Flesh; ✠ He Who to save our race, out-done through your malice, "humbled Himself, becoming obedient even unto death." He Who has built His Church on the firm rock and declared that the gates of hell shall not prevail against her, because He dwells with her "all days even to the consummation of the world." The hidden virtue of the Cross ✠ requires it of you as does also the power of the mysteries of the Christian Faith. ✠ The glorious Mother of God, the Virgin Mary commands you; ✠ she who by her humility and from the first moment of her Immaculate Conception crushed your proud head. The faith of the holy Apostles Peter and Paul, and of the other Apostles, commands you. ✠ The blood of the martyrs and the pious intercession of all the Saints command you. ✠ Thus, cursed dragon, and you wicked legions, we adjure you by the living God, ✠ by the true God, ✠ by the holy God, ✠ by God "Who so loved the world that He delivered His only Son that every soul believing in Him might not perish but have life everlasting." Cease deceiving human creatures and pouring out to them the poison of eternal perdition; cease harming the Church and hindering her liberty. Retreat, Satan, inventor and master of all deceit, enemy of man's salvation. Cede the place to Christ in Whom you have found none of your works.

Cede the place to the One, Holy, Catholic, and Apostolic Church acquired by Christ at the price of His Blood. Stoop beneath the all-powerful Hand of God, tremble and flee at the invocation of the holy and terrible Name of Jesus, this Name which causes hell to tremble, this Name to which the Virtues, Powers and Dominations of heaven are humbly submissive, this Name which the Cherubim and Seraphim praise unceasingly repeating: Holy, Holy, Holy, is the Lord, the God of Hosts.

V. O Lord hear my prayer.
R. And let my cry come unto Thee.
V. May the Lord be with you.
R. And with thy spirit.

LET US PRAY

God of heaven, God of earth, God of angels, God of Archangels, God of Patriarchs, God of Prophets, God of Apostles, God of Martyrs, God of Confessors, God of Virgins, God Who hast power to give life after death and rest after work; because there is no other God than Thou and there can be no other, for Thou art the Creator of all things, visible and invisible, of Whose reign there shall be no end, we humbly prostrate ourselves before Thy Glorious Majesty and we supplicate Thee to deliver us from all the tyranny of the infernal spirits, from their snares and their furious wickedness. Deign, O Lord, to protect us by Thy power and to preserve us safe and sound. We beseech Thee through Jesus Christ our Lord. Amen.

From the snares of the devil. *Deliver us, O Lord.*
That Thy Church may serve Thee in peace and liberty.
We beseech Thee to hear us.
That Thou mayest crush down all enemies of Thy Church.
We beseech Thee to hear us.

(Holy water is sprinkled in the place where we may be.)

Printed in Great Britain
by Amazon